Bada Bing!

Published in 2024 by OH!
An Imprint of Welbeck Non-Fiction Limited,
part of Welbeck Publishing Group.
Offices in: London – 20 Mortimer Street, London W1T 3JW
and Sydney – Level 17, 207 Kent St, Sydney NSW 2000 Australia
www.welbeckpublishing.com

Disclaimer:
All trademarks, company names, brand names, registered names, quotations,
scripted text,characters, logos, dialogues and catchphrases used or cited in this
book are the property of their respective owners and are mentioned in this
book within quotation fair dealings or used as cultural references or for identity,
review and guidance purpose only. The publisher does not assume and hereby
disclaim any liability to any party for any loss, damage or disruption caused
by errors or omissions, whether such errors or omissions result from negligence,
accident or any other cause. This book is a publication of *OH! An imprint of
Welbeck Publishing Group Limited* and has not been licensed, approved,
sponsored, or endorsed by any person or entity.

The Sopranos trademark and copyright are the property of
Home Box Office, Inc.

ISBN 978-1-80069-559-7

Compiled and written by: Victoria Godden
Editorial: Matt Tomlinson
Project manager: Russell Porter
Design: Tony Seddon
Production: Jess Brisley

A CIP catalogue record for this book is available from the British Library

Printed in China

10 9 8 7 6 5 4 3 2 1

Bada Bing!

THE LITTLE GUIDE TO
THE SOPRANOS

CONTENTS

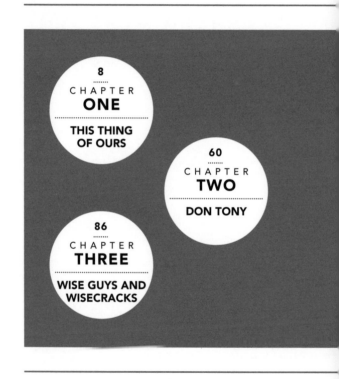

INTRODUCTION

When *The Sopranos* aired in 1999, it was at the forefront of what is now known as the Golden Age of Television, ushering in a new era of high-quality tragi-dramas that delighted critics and audiences alike.

Revolving around a suburban New Jersey mob boss, Tony Soprano, who employs the use of a psychiatrist in order to cope with his attempts to juggle work and home life, it is no exaggeration to say that the show redefined the crime drama genre. Instead of stereotypical mobsters with no conscience, *The Sopranos* stunned audiences with its sensitive portrayal of deeply flawed yet complex characters, each of which have their own hang-ups and insecurities, dreams and desires, as well as a very specific – albeit unconventional – code of ethics and morality.

THE
Sopranos

Plotlines are dark and twisting, dealing with complex themes of depression, suicide, family strife and betrayal, and yet *The Sopranos* never fails to find the lighter moments in amongst it all. In fact, it is streaked through with raucous humour and some truly unforgettable one-liners – some of the best of which you'll find in this book.

To celebrate the 25th anniversary of the show's premiere, *The Little Guide to The Sopranos* gives fans a chance to relive the magic, to remember some of its most indelible moments and pithy exchanges, as well as encounter some lesser-known trivia along the way. If nothing else, it'll give you a break from wondering about what really happened at that diner in the final scene.

So, let's grab some gabagool and get stuck in…

CHAPTER ONE

THIS THING OF OURS

First, let's take a look at how
The Sopranos all began,
twenty-five years ago…

The show premiered on HBO
on 10 January 1999.

The pilot was called simply
"The Sopranos".

THE
Sopranos

Creator David Chase originally pitched his concept of the Soprano family as a movie about a gangster going to therapy to talk about issues he was having with his mother.

His manager, Lloyd Braun, thought it had potential for a TV series instead.

I want you to know that
we believe that you have
inside you a great television
series.

Lloyd Braun, David Chase's manager

THE
Sopranos

The Sopranos was turned down by Fox network after they read the script for the pilot because they thought the therapy angle would be too challenging for audiences.

They came in here and said, 'Here's the idea: 40-year-old guy, crossroads of his life, turmoil in his marriage, turmoil in his professional career, beginning to raise teenage kids in modern society – all the pressures of every man in his generation. The only difference is he's the Mob boss of northern New Jersey. Oh, by the way, he's seeing a shrink.

Richard Plepler, co-president of HBO, on the initial pitch for *The Sopranos*, as quoted in *Vanity Fair*, "The Family Hour: An Oral History of *The Sopranos*", by Annie Liebovitz and Sam Kashner, 15 March 2012.

THE Sopranos

The name "Soprano" was the family name of a boy David Chase met as a child, through his father's business partner.

The theme song for *The Sopranos* is "Woke Up This Morning" by Alabama 3, from their album *Exile on Coldharbour Lane*.

The show uses a shortened version of the "Chosen One Mix" of the song.

THE Sopranos

Originally, David Chase wanted to
use a different song in the opening
credits to each episode, but the other
producers convinced him otherwise.

As a concession of sorts, he did
get to use a different song at the end
of each episode.

The house that Tony and his
family live in for the duration of the
show is in North Caldwell,
and can also be seen in the famous
opening credits.

THE Sopranos

Chase only directed two episodes of the show: the first and the last.

Most of the episodes were directed by Tim Van Patten, while others who took directorial turns include Allen Coulter, Steve Buscemi and Lorraine Senna.

Chase's original pick for the actor playing the part of Tony Soprano was Steven Van Zandt, a guitar player in Bruce Springsteen's E Street Band.

Fortunately for James Gandolfini, the producers didn't want to take the risk on a first-time actor for the lead role, and so Chase created the part of Silvio Dante for Van Zandt instead.

THE Sopranos

Silvio's wife, Gabriella, was actually played by Van Zandt's real-life wife, Maureen.

In order to prepare for the role, Van Zandt employed the tailor of real-life mafia boss John Gotti to make clothes for his character.

He also gained 70lb.

THE Sopranos

> **66**
>
> I decided that I had to create this guy. … And part of the biography, by the way, was that he kind of romanticized the mob's history and felt that the best times were over. … But he was a traditionalist, so he wanted to have that kind of honor that he felt the old mob guys had, and so he looked like a throwback. I have a Fifties haircut and a Fifties kind of demeanor, because that was his philosophy.
>
> **99**

Van Zandt on Silvio's character motivations and unique look, *Rolling Stone* interview with Andy Greene, 7 January 2020

James Gandolfini got the part
of Tony after casting director
Susan Fitzgerald saw a clip of him
in the 1993 film *True Romance*.

I thought that they would hire some good-looking guy, not George Clooney, but some Italian George Clooney, and that would be that.

James Gandolfini on his expectations for the casting of Tony Soprano, as quoted in the *New Yorker*, "Postscript: James Gandolfini, 1961–2013" by David Remnick, 19 June 2013.

As well as Steven Van Zandt,
other actors who auditioned for the
role of Tony Soprano include
Ray Liotta, Anthony LaPaglia and
Michael Pispoli.

THE
Sopranos

Ray Liotta was actually offered the part of Ralphie later on, but turned it down.

Later he would agree to star alongside James Gandolfini's son, Michael, for the Sopranos prequel, *The Many Saints of Newark*.

Lorraine Bracco, who plays Tony's therapist Dr Jennifer Melfi, was originally asked to play Tony's wife, Carmela.

She turned down the part because she deemed it too similar to her role in *Goodfellas*, in which she played gangster Henry Hill's wife Karen.

THE Sopranos

"

I was not ready for how
fucking difficult Dr. Melfi was
to play. I am an explosive girl.
I am loud. I am full of life and
full of all kinds of bullshit, and
I have to sit on every emotion,
every word, everything, to play
this character.

"

Lorraine Bracco, on the challenges of her chosen role

In the end the part of Tony's wife Carmela went to Edie Falco, who had actually expected to be given the part of Dr Melfi.

She went on to win three Primetime Emmy Awards for her performance.

THE
Sopranos

"

Carmela was very easy to be. I immediately knew how she felt about things, the way she wanted to look. But an Italian-American Mob wife? I'm not the first person I would think of. I would have cast me as Dr. Melfi, but, luckily, I was not in charge.

"

Edie Falco, as quoted in *Vanity Fair*, "The Family Hour: An Oral History of *The Sopranos*", by Annie Liebovitz and Sam Kashner, 15 March 2012.

The Sopranos features 27 actors that also appear in Martin Scorsese's mobster film of 1990, *Goodfellas*, including regular cast members Lorraine Bracco (Jennifer Melfi), Michael Imperioli (Christopher Moltisanti), Tony Sirico (Paulie Gaultieri), Vincent Pastore (Salvatore "Big Pussy" Bonpensiero), Frank Vincent (Phil Leotardo), and Joseph R. Gannascoli (Vito Spatafore).

Sopranos

Other mafia films are referenced constantly in *The Sopranos* – including *Goodfellas* and *The Godfather*.

In fact, the name of the strip club, Bada Bing, is borrowed from a phrase that was ad-libbed and used repeatedly by James Caan's character, Sonny Corleone, in *The Godfather*.

They brought me in, and I met with David [Chase]. I thought he hated my audition, because David's a poker-faced guy. He kept giving me notes and giving me direction, and I walked out of there, and I was like, 'I blew that one.'

Michael Imperioli, remembering his audition for the role of Christopher Moltisanti – wrongly, as it turned out…

THE
Sopranos

Drea de Matteo, who plays Christopher's girlfriend Adriana, almost didn't get cast in the role.

David Chase didn't think she was Italian enough for the part and looked more like a server in a restaurant – which is why she appears in one scene of the pilot as an unnamed waitress at Vesuvio's – the restaurant frequented by Tony and his friends and owned by Artie Bucco and his wife Charmaine.

It was only later, when she show got picked up, that she was invited back to audition for the role of Adriana.

She ended up winning a Primetime Emmy for her performance in 2004.

THE Sopranos

"

At this point I knew what I was dealing with. So I wore my nameplate in diamonds. I teased my hair up a little bit. One of the words in the line was 'Ow,' and the reason that I got the part was because the way I said 'Owwuhwhwwwuhwwwuh!' I turned it into, like, five syllables.

"

Drea de Matteo, as quoted in *Vanity Fair*, "The Family Hour: An Oral History of *The Sopranos*", by Annie Liebovitz and Sam Kashner, 15 March 2012.

"

Chris-ta-fuh!

"

Once you've heard the way Adriana says her fiancé's name, you can't unhear it...

THE Sopranos

66

I felt like my accent sounded so forced and I hated saying it. So I went to David Chase and I said: 'I can't say Christopher like that all the time, can I call him Chrissy?' If you notice throughout the series I pepper it with Chrissy and Christopher.

99

Drea de Matteo on how she got around saying "Christopher" all the time, interview with *NME*, 6 April 2021.

Before he played Paulie "Walnuts" Gaultieri, Tony Sirico was a (not-so-) honest-to-goodness criminal, and much of his character's storyline came from events straight out of his life.

He agreed to be in the show on the condition that his character never be a "rat" (i.e. become an informer for the Feds).

THE **Sopranos**

“

I lived with Ma for 16 years before she passed. David knew that going in. That became one of my story lines.

”

Tony Sirico

Tony Sirico originally auditioned
for the role of Corrado
"Uncle Junior" Soprano, which went
to Dominic Chianese.

THE
Sopranos

"

That helped me tremendously –
subconsciously at first and then
consciously. After the first couple of
seasons I couldn't act without them.
They were part of my makeup.
Those glasses were my mask. We were
doing Greek tragedy there. Behind
the mask a lot of things come out that
you wouldn't do.

"

After Dominic Chianese's audition, he was sat in a room
with different kinds of glasses.

As quoted in *Vanity Fair*, "The Family Hour: An Oral
History of *The Sopranos*", by Annie Liebovitz and
Sam Kashner, 15 March 2012.

Most of the filming was
done at Silvercup Studios in Queens,
New York City, and on location
in New Jersey.

THE Sopranos

After filming ended, the iconic
Satriale's Pork Store at
101 Kearny Avenue, New Jersey,
was demolished.

"

A don doesn't wear shorts.

"

Carmine Lupertazzi

^{THE}Sopranos

The advice not to wear shorts,
given to Tony Soprano in the
first episode of Season 4, was actually
given to the writers by real mobsters,
who had taken exception to the
character's wardrobe choices.

In Season 4, the cast got into
a contract dispute with HBO over
their salaries.

To settle it, James Gandolfini
reputedly gave each of the 16 main
actors a cheque for $33,000.

THE Sopranos

When asked about this years later,
actor Steven Van Zandt (who played
Silvio Dante) said that, in fact,
"It wasn't to settle a salary dispute.
He had gotten a big raise
and just divided it amongst the cast.
He was one of a kind."

David Chase liked to keep both
the actors guessing right along with
audiences when it came to plotlines –
especially when it came to whether
or not they were 'whacked'.

Drea de Matteo filmed two endings
for her character Adriana, so she
was just as surprised as we were when
her demise came to light…

Sopranos

Similarly, Vincent Pastore, the actor who plays Salvatore "Big Pussy" Bonpensiero, wasn't told that he was actually an FBI informant until it was revealed to the other characters in the show.

The Sopranos finale, entitled "Made in America", aired on 10 June 2007, and the last four minutes are widely considered to constitute one of the most controversial and ambiguous endings to a TV series ever.

THE
Sopranos

In the final scene, Tony waits in a diner for Carmela, Meadow and AJ, putting Journey's "Don't Stop Believin'" on the jukebox. Carmela arrives, followed by AJ, and they get started on some onion rings while they wait for Meadow, who's attempting to parallel park outside.

We hear the sound of a bell – presumably Meadow or someone else entering the diner – which makes Tony look up, and then the screen suddenly cuts to black, leaving audiences literally in the dark about what happens next.

When the final scene aired,
many viewers thought their cable
had cut out at the most
critical point in the show – only
to realize afterwards that, no,
that really was the end.

THE Sopranos

66

'When I first saw the ending,
I said, 'What the fuck.' I mean,
after all I went through, all this
death, and then it's over like
that? After I had a day to sleep,
I just sat there and said:
'That's perfect.'

99

James Gandolfini on the series finale

Fans are divided into two camps – those who believe Tony was killed (probably by the guy who had gone into the bathroom moments before), and that the cut to black signified the end of his consciousness, and those who aren't so sure.

THE
Sopranos

There are several illusions to death
earlier on in the episode,
including how Tony appears to be
dead in the opening scene (while in
fact he's actually just asleep) and all
that crazy weather, but also in the
final season generally.

66

You probably don't even hear it when it happens, right?

99

Bobby Bacala raises the question of what happens when you die in the season 6 premiere – and his question is sadly answered in the affirmative by the penultimate episode…

THE
Sopranos

Despite being a series, each
episode of *The Sopranos* is noted
for its cinematic look, and this
was down to David Chase and
director of photography Alik Sakharov,
who together would break each
scene down into shots.

Alik Sakharov would go on to direct
episodes of *House of Cards*, *Ozark*,
and *Game of Thrones*.

CHAPTER TWO

DON TONY

All things Tony Soprano – the
undisputed boss of television.

It's good to be in something from the ground floor. I came too late for that, I know. But lately, I'm getting the feeling that I came in at the end. The best is over.

Tony Soprano muses on life as a modern-day mobster with his therapist

THE Sopranos

66

This psychiatry shit. Apparently what you're feeling is not what you're feeling and what you're not feeling is your real agenda.

99

Tony Soprano gets frustrated with his therapy sessions

Tony starts therapy with Dr Melfi after having a panic attack, which he believes are caused by the stress of having to hide the nature of his job, however the real reason is revealed later on.

THE Sopranos

In Season 3's episode
"Fortunate Son", we learn that
Tony's first ever panic attack
happened when he was just a child,
after witnessing his father
cut a butcher's finger off over
an unpaid debt.

They take home some free
cold cuts, and Tony faints when he
sees his mother happily cutting
into the meat, with no concern about
how it was procured.

Whatever happened to Gary Cooper? The strong, silent type. … He wasn't in touch with his feelings. He just did what he had to do.

Tony wonders why everyone needs to talk about their feelings so much these days…

^{THE} Sopranos

James Gandolfini is the only
cast member that appears in every
episode of *The Sopranos*.

66

You don't shit where you eat. And you really don't shit where I eat.

99

Tony Soprano gives Benny Fazio a motto he'd do well to live by

---

"

What do you want, an
apology? A fucking Whitman
Sampler? What?

"

A brilliant example of Tony's trash-talking – this time
directed at Johnny Sack

Tony was born "Anthony John Soprano", and he started his criminal career under his uncle and mentor Dickie Moltisanti.

He committed his first murder in his early twenties, that of Willie Overall, under the tutelage of his father's friend — Paulie "Walnuts" Gualtieri.

All due respect, you got no fucking idea what it's like to be Number One. Every decision you make affects every facet of every other fucking thing. It's too much to deal with almost. And in the end, you're completely alone with it all.

"

Tony confides in consigliere Sil about the stresses of leadership

---

"

Those who want respect
give respect.

"

Tony explains how "This Thing of Ours" really works

Between Season 1 and 2,
Tony is promoted from a capo to
street boss of the DiMeo crime
family, after his uncle Junior is retired
after shooting Tony.

THE Sopranos

> **"** We're soldiers. Soldiers don't go to hell. **"**

Tony tries to justify his livelihood to Dr Melfi

"
If you can quote the rules,
then you can obey them.
"

Tony reminds Paulie about mafia code

THE Sopranos

"

But you should know he never wanted this life for you. And I'll tell you something: I don't want it for my son either.

"

Tony tries to convince Jackie Aprile Jr to get out of the family business, and that his father wanted him to be a doctor

Tony authorizes the killing of
twelve people during the course of
The Sopranos, however he is also
directly responsible for eight
murders – that we know of.

66

How come I'm not making pots
in Peru? You're born to this shit.
You are what you are.

99

Tony tells Dr Melfi what he thinks about the concept of
free will

Last week I called you a whore.
I might have been ... overstating
the case a little bit.

Tony apologizes to Dr Melfi for some harsh words –
sort of…

ᵀᴴᴱ Sopranos

To get into the Tony Soprano mindset, James Gandolfini reportedly put rocks in his shoes to make him uncomfortable.

He would also stay up all night before shooting scenes in which Tony was supposed to be sleep-deprived.

Well, when you're married, you'll understand the importance of fresh produce.

Tony gives Christopher some advice on relationships…

THE
Sopranos

Tony was notorious for his
affairs with women other than his
wife, Carmela.

As well as one-night stands
with the strippers at his club,
Bada Bing, he also has a series of
mistresses during the show.

"

You should try 'Tomato Sauce for Your Ass' – it's the Italian version.

"

Tony isn't impressed with his girlfriend's book choice, *Chicken Soup for the Soul*

THE Sopranos

"

I'm like King Midas in reverse
here. Everything I touch
turns to shit.

"

Tony Soprano just can't catch a break

CHAPTER THREE

WISE GUYS AND WISECRACKS

When it comes to the wit
and wisdom to be found in
The Sopranos, audiences are
truly spoiled for choice…

"

As far as f***ing bears are concerned, I say, get rid of them all. They had their turn, and now we got ours. That's why dinosaurs don't exist no more.

"

Paulie Gualtieri

THE Sopranos

❝

Your mother was working
the bonbon concession at
the Eiffel Tower.

❞

Paulie Gualtieri

When I was a kid, you two were old ladies. Now I'm old, and you two are still old.

Paulie Gualtieri lovingly roasts his mother's friends

THE Sopranos

66

One time we saw a sign
that said 'bear left', so we
went home.

99

Bobby makes a bear joke while reminiscing about hunting
trips with his family while him and Tony go to rescue
Paulie and Christopher in the Pine Barrens

"

Paulie: You're not gonna believe this. The guy killed 16 Czechoslovakians. He was an interior decorator.
Christopher: His house looked like shit.

"

Paulie Gualtieri mishears Tony warning about Valery, who killed 16 Chechen rebels and was once in the Russian Interior Ministry... to great comedic effect

THE Sopranos

66

Carmela: I'm not giving you my engagement ring. This isn't stolen.
Tony: …
Carmela: Is it?

99

Carmela, ever naïve about the proceeds of crime!

More is lost by indecision than by wrong decision.

Carmela Soprano

"

Other people's definitions of you, sometimes they're more about making themselves feel better. You gotta define yourself.

"

Christopher Moltisanti

You heard about the Chinese Godfather? He made them an offer they couldn't understand.

Corrado "Junior" Soprano

THE Sopranos

Silvio: [seeing a beautiful woman across the street] I could do that, no problem.
Christopher: Wait here, I'll get your Viagra.

Christopher couldn't resist mocking Silvio and his sexual "prowess"…

Last year I made bail so fast, my soup was still warm when I got home.

Silvio expertly mocks the FBI at the funeral shake-down

THE Sopranos

"

Take it easy. We're not
making a Western here.

"

Junior effectively puts down Mickey Palmice when he
suggests killing Christopher to send a message

'Remember when' is the lowest form of conversation.

Tony Soprano really knows how to shut down a bit of idle chit-chat

THE Sopranos

> **66**
> What did you guys do
> for 12 hours? Play 'Name
> that Pope'?
> **99**

Tony mocks Carmela about her evening with her priest

He's a good-looking kid.
Sure he's yours?

Tony jokes with Big Pussy about his son

THE Sopranos

> **What constitutes a fidget?**

Tony finds it hard to grasp his son's potential ADD diagnosis

That's okay. We have to break our dependency on foreign oil.

AJ has a brilliant response to his dad refusing to buy him a new car

THE Sopranos

> **"**
> Every day is a gift. But does it have to be a pair of socks?
> **"**

Tony talks frankly about how hard it is to enjoy life as a gangster in a frank conversation with Dr Melfi

Even a broken clock is right twice a day.

Another of Tony's classic put-downs…

THE Sopranos

66

Teddy Roosevelt once gave an entire speech with a bullet lodged in his chest. Some things are just a matter of duty.

99

Junior Soprano

Some people are so far behind in a race that they actually believe they're leading.

Junior Soprano

THE Sopranos

66

You steer the ship the best way you know, sometimes it's smooth, sometimes you hit the rocks.

99

Junior Soprano gives some good life advice

You're only as good as your last envelope.

Silvio Dante gives some business wisdom

THE Sopranos

> **"**
>
> Oh, Mickey Blue Eyes, you're home. Qu'est-ce que c'est? Answering machine broken?
>
> **"**

Artie tries – and fails – to appear tough on a debt-collection mission

Paulie: "I can't believe this."
Ralph: Why not? Last year you believed there was a flying saucer over East Rutherford.

Ralph loves nothing more than mocking Paulie, on this occasion his tendency to believe in conspiracy theories

I had some problems with my screenplay, so I bought that book, *How to Write a Movie in 21 Days*. That was like a year ago.

Christopher Moltisanti fails to hear his own words – as usual…

Fear knocked at the door.
Faith answered. There was
no one there.

99

Christopher Moltisanti

66

Life's too short. You can't waste it fighting with your friends.

99

Paulie Gualtieri

Dr Melfi: I have patients who are suicidal!

Tony Soprano: Well they're not gonna feel any better about their life if you get clipped.

Tony states the obvious somewhat while trying to convince Dr Melfi to go into hiding for her own safety

THE
Sopranos

66

Death just shows the
ultimate absurdity of life.

99

AJ tries to school his parents in morality

CHAPTER FOUR

NEVER EAT ALONE

From family dinners to fast food, not forgetting those life-saving ketchup packets, this chapter gives a voice to the uncredited cast member of *The Sopranos*: Food.

66

Let's eat!

99

Carmela knows how to please a crowd at AJ's birthday party in the pilot episode.

THE Sopranos

One of Tony's offices is at
the back of Satriale's Pork Store, an
Italian meat market in New Jersey.

It has a coffee bar at the front that
sells pasties and is often
frequented by the Soprano
crime family.

Satriale's veal parmesan sandwiches
are a favourite of FBI agent
Dwight Harris, and Silvio's wife is a
fan of their gabagool (or capicola,
a pork cold cut).

^{THE} Sopranos

66

Gabagool? Over here!!

99

Silvio is never one to say no to gabagool

66

All this from a slice of gabagool?

99

Tony doesn't buy Dr Melfi's professional take on his childhood memories

---

66

It's almost time for turkey sandwiches!

99

When Janice brings a narcoleptic to dinner, Tony can't resist poking fun as he falls asleep at the table

---

Pizza is often the meal of choice for bonding sessions between Tony and his son, AJ.

However, when AJ and his friends break into their high school and go swimming, police are able to identify the culprits from the custom pizza remains.

> **"**
>
> That's a custom job …
> Double meatball, peperoni,
> sausage, peppers, onions,
> extra moozadell.
>
> **"**

AJ's love of signature toppings gets him in hot water with the police

---

Baked ziti, a classic American pasta bake made with cheese and a tomato-based sauce similar to a bolognese, plays a prominent role in *The Sopranos*.

THE Sopranos

"

No fucking ziti?!

"

AJ is very upset when his grandmother decides not to come to his birthday – and therefore won't be bringing her famous baked ziti with her…

66

Karen's ziti?

99

When Bobby's wife Karen dies, Janice tries to insert herself into his life, the pinnacle of which is this moment, when she coerces him into eating the last meal Karen made and put in the freezer before she died – baked ziti.

THE Sopranos

Phil: I also have a confession to make, Carm. I have a jones for your baked ziti.

Carmela: Sure, anytime. I have some in the freezer right now. I can reheat it.

Phil: It's so much better that way, isn't it? The moozadel' gets all nice and chewy.

Carmela: I like that too.

Father Phil and Carmela bond over their love of reheated baked ziti…

Is there a commandment against eating ziti?

Carmela tries to assuage her guilt about her semi-chaste evening with Father Phil

THE Sopranos

Friggin' olive oil. The food was drenched. That's why this happened.

Silvio

66

Not bad! Mix it with the relish.

99

When Christopher and Paulie get stranded in the Pine Barrens, some stray condiment packets from an old bag of fast-food left inside an abandoned van become their lifeline…

THE Sopranos

> **Christopher:** What are those? Tic Tacs?
>
> **Paulie:** I just found them, I didn't know I had them on me.
>
> **Christopher:** You had Tic Tacs all along? Give me some.
>
> **Paulie:** There ain't no more, I ate them.
>
> **Christopher:** Selfish prick. I'm dying here.
>
> **Paulie:** Then fuckin die already.

Paulie decides not to share his Tic Tacs in the Pine Barrens – much to Christopher's irritation...

Vesuvio's, the restaurant owned by
Artie Bucco and his wife, is one
of the regular haunts of the Soprano
family and provides a backdrop for
a lot of the drama of the show.

Sopranos

> **Tony:** What the fuck is that?
> **Artie:** Quail, a la Bucco.
> Baby quail stuffed with
> fennel sausage.

It's not mozzarella. This is called burrata. I had it flown in this morning by FedEx from Italy. It's a lot more subtle and smooth than mozzarella with an almost nut-like flavor.

Artie tries to educate Carmela and Rosalie about the delicacy that is burrata.

THE Sopranos

66

Cavalry's here. I brought some cannelloni.

99

Artie comes to the rescue with food when Tony gets shot by his uncle and ends up in hospital

---

66

Classless pieces of shit.

99

The locals don't think much of Paulie's request for "macaroni and gravy" (red sauce) when he visits Naples with Tony and Christopher …

Goddam Orange Peel Beef.

Woe betide anyone who gets Tony's takeout order wrong...

I know this is hard for you to believe, but food may not be the answer to every problem.

AJ Soprano tells his mother some hard truths when she offers to make him French toast to make him feel better after a breakup

THE Sopranos

> **"**
> I went ahead and ordered
> some for the table.
> **"**

If we needed any more confirmation – the last line of
the show epitomises food's central role in the lives of
its characters, and gives us a final insight into Tony's
overarching motivation: to put food on his family's table –
well, onion rings, in this case.

CHAPTER FIVE

THE FAMILY

At its heart, *The Sopranos* was a show about family – the mothers and sons, fathers and daughters, sibling rivalries and all those "Uncles", naturally…

The show's original premise
was based on Tony's strained
relationship with his mother, Livia
Soprano, which provided much
of the tension of the first series.

THE Sopranos

"

What kind of person can
I be, where his own mother
wants him dead?

"

Tony Soprano

> **"**
> # My son, the mental patient.
> **"**

Livia is eternally embarrassed by Tony's therapy sessions

THE
Sopranos

Originally, David Chase intended for Tony to succeed in suffocating his mother with a pillow at the end of the first season.

However, Nancy Marchland, the actress who played Livia, was sick at the time and asked David to keep her working, which Chase did.

"

He goes to talk about his mother. That's what he's doing. He talks about me, he complains. 'She didn't do this, she did that.' Oh, I gave my life to my children on a silver platter, and this is how he repays me.

"

Livia Soprano

Livia Soprano was a character based
on David Chase's own mother.

Daughters are better at taking care of their mothers than sons.

Livia Soprano can never resist a dig at Tony

THE Sopranos

> **Livia:** I know your father doesn't let you come down here.
>
> **AJ:** That's not true. He just doesn't want us to talk about you in the house.
>
> **Livia:** He can go shit in his hat.

Livia, a loving mother and grandmother as always…

Now that my father's dead, he's a saint. When he was alive? Nothing.

Tony Soprano marvels at his mother's memory of his father

THE Sopranos

"

They're the vehicle that gets us here. They drop us off and go on their way. They continue on their journey. And the problem is that we keep trying to get back on the bus, instead of just letting it go.

"

Tony Soprano muses about the death of his parents

Carmela: You know what I want, Tony? I want those kids to have a father.

Tony: They got one. This one. Me. Tony Soprano. And all that comes with it.

99

THE Sopranos

66

Why does everything have to be so hard? I'm not saying I'm perfect but I do the right thing by my family. Doesn't that count for anything?

99

Tony Soprano

You know, Tony, it's a multiple-choice thing with you. 'Cause I can't tell if you're old-fashioned, you're paranoid, or just a fucking asshole.

99

Carmela Soprano wonders about which of these afflictions is the root cause of her husband's temperament

THE Sopranos

66

Tony: AJ, go see who's at the door.

AJ: I'm eating.

Tony: Yeah but you won't have any teeth left to eat with if you don't get up off your ass and see who's at the door.

99

Tony models some top-notch parenting with his son, AJ

That's the guy, Adriana.
My Uncle Tony. The guy I'm
going to hell for.

Christopher Moltisanti

THE Sopranos

Tony refers to Christopher as his nephew throughout the show, but in fact he is Carmela's first cousin once removed, and only a cousin through marriage to Tony.

However, because Tony was so close to Christopher's father, Dickie, and has acted like a father to Christopher, they call each other 'nephew' and 'uncle'.

When Christopher shoots an employee of a bakery in the foot, this is a reference to Michael Imperioli being shot in the foot by Joe Pesci in his role in *Goodfellas*.

THE Sopranos

"

I don't care how close you are: in the end, your friends are gonna let you down. Family. They're the only ones you can depend on.

"

Tony Soprano encapsulates the idea that blood is always thicker than water

66

For every 20 wrongs a child does, ignore 19.

99

Janice Soprano on parenting

THE Sopranos

"

Carmela: What kind of animal smokes marijuana at his own confirmation?

AJ: I don't know.

Carmela: Be a good Catholic for fifteen fucking minutes; is that so much to ask?!

"

Carmela struggles with her son's behaviour

66

Dad, are you in the mafia?

99

Meadow Soprano gets to the heart of the issue on their college road trip

THE Sopranos

66

Why can't this family just get along?

99

Meadow Soprano asks the question most families ask themselves at some point or another!

❝

Meadow: Dad, I've lived in the house all my life. I've seen the police come with warrants. I've seen you going out at three in the morning.

Tony: So you never seen Doc Cusamano going out at three in the morning on a call?

Meadow: Did the Cusamano kids ever find $50,000 in krugerrands and a .45 automatic while they were hunting for Easter eggs?

❞

Not much gets past Meadow Soprano…

THE Sopranos

66

A grown man made a wager.
He lost. He made another one –
he lost again. End of story.

99

Tony gives Meadow a lesson in the school of hard knocks

Someday soon you're gonna have families of your own, and if you're lucky, you'll remember the little moments like this that were good.

Tony Soprano's fatherly words of wisdom

THE
Sopranos

The *Sopranos* boasts an alumni
that went on to amazing things:
executive producer Matthew Weiner
created *Mad Men*, executive producer
Terence Winter created *Boardwalk
Empire*, while Tim Van Patten directed
episodes of *Boardwalk Empire* and
Game of Thrones.

Writers Robin Green and Mitchell
Burgess created *Blue Bloods*,
and Todd A. Kessler was one of the
creators of *Damages*.

CHAPTER SIX

IT'S A HIT

Awards and accolades, records
and wider cultural influence

The Sopranos ran for 6 seasons –
86 episodes in total.

THE Sopranos

In 2004, *The Sopranos* became the first cable TV show to win the Emmy Award for Outstanding Drama Series, having been nominated for the award five times previously.

It was nominated every year subsequently, until it won again for its final, sixth season in 2007.

The Sopranos earned a whopping
112 Emmy nominations
during its time on air – 21 of which
it won.

^{THE} Sopranos

22.6 million viewers tuned in for the 2001 season premiere.

Until that point, no other show had ever topped 20 million.

In 2016, *Rolling Stone* named
The Sopranos the best TV show
of all time.

THE Sopranos

> ... nearly two decades after it faded to black in a Jersey diner with the jukebox playing 'Don't Stop Believin', The Sopranos remains the standard all ambitious TV aspires to meet.

Rolling Stone

The show was so realistic that,
when it came out, real-life organized
crime families were recorded by the
FBI discussing it, convinced there
must be an informer in the crew.

THE Sopranos

"

Is that supposed to be us?

"

Members of the DeCavalcante crime family wonder whether they are the inspiration for the fictional New Jersey crime family of *The Sopranos*

Sopranos gave the lie to the notions that you had to explain everything, that you always had to have a star in the lead, that everybody had to be ultimately likable, that there had to be so-called closure, that there was a psychological lesson to be learned, that there was a moral at the center that you should carry away from the show, that people should be pretty, that people should be svelte.

Allen Coulter, director, as quoted in *Vanity Fair*, "The Family Hour: An Oral History of *The Sopranos*", by Annie Liebovitz and Sam Kashner, 15 March 2012.

THE Sopranos

The Sopranos paved the way for what is now known as "prestige TV". Here are some of the shows that owe it a debt of gratitude:

Sons of Anarchy	*Gomorrah*
Ray Donovan	*Brotherhood*
Magic City	*Breaking Bad*
Mad Men	*Boardwalk Empire*
Lilyhammer	*The Americans*

"10 TV Shows that are clearly inspired by *The Sopranos*" by Devin Meenan, cbr.com

---

The Sopranos is so good, if I had to choose between watching *The Sopranos* and breathing, I'd pause ... think about it ... then watch another episode.

99

Saturday Night Live spoofs *The Sopranos'* ecstatic reviews

THE SOPRANOS

In the *Simpsons* episode
"Poppa's Got a Brand New Badge"
(2002), the mafia drive through
Springfield to the song "Woke Up
This Morning" by Alabama 3, parodying
the intro to *The Sopranos*.

In 2006, a video game based on
The Sopranos was released.

The Sopranos: Road to Respect
takes place sometime between
Season 5 and 6, and the player
takes the role of Joey LaRocca, the
illegitimate son of Salvatore
"Big Pussy" Bonpensiero.

The Sopranos

The 10 best Sopranos episodes according to IMBD

1. Pine Barrens – S.3, E.11

2. The Blue Comet – S.6, E.20

3. Long Term Parking – S.5, E.12

4. Funhouse – S.2, E.13

5. Made in America – S.6, E.21

6. Whoever Did This – S.4, E.9

7. The Knight in White Satin Armor – S.2, E.12

8. Whitecaps – S.4, E.13

9. All Due Respect – S.5, E.13

10. The Second Coming – S.6, E.19

On 19 June 2013,
James Gandolfini died of a heart attack
while in Rome, aged 51.

THE
Sopranos

"

We're all in shock and feeling immeasurable sadness at the loss of a beloved member of our family. He was a special man, a great talent, but more importantly a gentle and loving person who treated everyone no matter their title or position with equal respect.

"

Statement from HBO after the death of James Gandolfini

The love between Tony and Carmela was one of the greatest I've ever known. I am shocked and devastated by Jim's passing. He was a man of tremendous depth and sensitivity, with a kindness and generosity beyond words. I consider myself very lucky to have spent 10 years as his close colleague. My heart goes out to his family. I will hold on to the memories of our intense and beautiful time together.

Edie Falco responds to the news of
James Gandolfini's death

THE
Sopranos

A prequel to *The Sopranos*,
the feature-length film *The Many Saints
of Newark* was released in 2021.

It starred James Gandolfini's son,
Michael, in the lead role as a young
Tony Soprano and centres around
a violent gang war that occurs in the
midst of Newark's 1967 riots.

The Many Saints of Newark
was not only a streaming success
in its own right, viewed 1 million
times in its opening weekend, but
renewed interest in *The Sopranos*,
which broke HBO Max
viewing records around the time of
Many Saints's release.